(Is this ... illo?

Sedaka and Howard Greenfield
arr. Alexander L'Estrange

4

-ging my pil - low, dream-ing dreams of A - ma - ril - lo,
-ging my pil - low, dream-ing dreams of A - ma - ril - lo,

and sweet Ma - rie who waits___ for me. Show me the way to A-
and sweet Ma - rie who waits___ for me. *bap ba da bap!* the way to A-

- ma - ril - lo. I've been weep-ing like___ a wil - low,
- ma - ril - lo. I've been weep-ing like___ a wil - low,

Dream a little dream of me

Words and music by Willy Schwandt, Fabian Andre and Gus Kahn
arr. Alexander L'Estrange

14

Can't take my eyes off you

Words and music by Bob Crewe and Bob Gaudio
arr. Alexander L'Estrange

2nd time to Coda (p. 23)

Oh pret - ty ba - by, don't bring me down I pray, oh pret - ty ba - by, now that I've found you, stay, And let me love you ba - by, let me love you

You're just too good to be true. Can't take my eyes off you,

bup doo wah bup bup doo wah, bup doo wah

You'd be like hea - ven to touch. I wan - na hold you so much.

bup bup doo wah, bup doo wah bup bup doo wah, ooh

choral basics

consultant editor Alexander L'Estrange

(Is this the way to) Amarillo?: this exciting collection comprises three well-loved retro classics that over time have captured hearts and imaginations everywhere. Enjoy the fresh arrangements of these timeless hits – '(Is this the way to) Amarillo?', 'Dream a little dream of me' and 'Can't take my eyes off you' – which inspire nostalgia for a bygone era.

● ● ● ● ● ● ● ●

choral basics has been carefully designed to provide rewarding, varied repertoire for beginner choirs. Perfect for singers of all ages, the series offers:

- simple choral arrangements for 2 parts (soprano and alto) and 3 parts (soprano, alto and a combined male-voice part)
- an array of repertoire including world music, spirituals, pop classics, show hits and original pieces
- attractive, idiomatic arrangements, with breathing and vocal range considered for the level
- straightforward piano accompaniments, supporting the vocal lines
- great value for money, with each volume comprising a set of contrasted songs for easy programming

So build up your confidence and kick-start your choral singing with **choral basics**!

Alexander L'Estrange

Also available in this series:

FABER *ff* MUSIC

fabermusic.com

ISBN10: 0-571-52618-7
EAN13: 978-0-571-52618-5

9 780571 526185